Why Do We Need Air?

Kelley MacAulay

Crabtree Publishing Company
www.crabtreebooks.com

Author
Kelley MacAulay

Publishing plan research and development
Reagan Miller

Notes to adults
Reagan Miller

Editor
Crystal Sikkens

Proofreader
Wendy Scavuzzo

Design
Tammy McGarr

Photo research
Tammy McGarr, Crystal Sikkens

**Production coordinator
and prepress technician**
Tammy McGarr

Print coordinator
Margaret Amy Salter

Photographs
Kekyalyaynen/Shutterstock: pages 16, 24
Thinkstock: pages 3, 9, 10 (left), 13, 20, 24
All other images by Shutterstock

Library and Archives Canada Cataloguing in Publication

MacAulay, Kelley, author
Why do we need air? / Kelley MacAulay.

(Natural resources close-up)
Includes index.
Issued in print and electronic formats.
ISBN 978-0-7787-0491-1 (bound).--ISBN 978-0-7787-0495-9 (pbk.).--
ISBN 978-1-4271-8216-6 (html).--ISBN 978-1-4271-8220-3 (pdf)

1. Air--Juvenile literature. I. Title.

QC161.2.M23 2014   j551.5   C2014-900377-3
                                          C2014-900378-1

Library of Congress Cataloging-in-Publication Data

MacAulay, Kelley.
Why do we need air? / Kelley MacAulay.
pages cm. -- (Natural resources close-up)
Includes index.
ISBN 978-0-7787-0491-1 (reinforced library binding : alk. paper) -- ISBN 978-0-
7787-0495-9 (pbk. : alk. paper) -- ISBN 978-1-4271-8216-6 (electronic html : alk.
paper) -- ISBN 978-1-4271-8220-3 (electronic pdf : alk. paper)
1. Air--Juvenile literature. I. Title.
QC161.2.M32 2014
333.9'2--dc23
                                          2014002276

Crabtree Publishing Company

www.crabtreebooks.com   1-800-387-7650

Printed in Canada/032016/CH20160307

Published in Canada
Crabtree Publishing
616 Welland Ave.
St. Catharines, Ontario
L2M 5V6

Published in the United States
Crabtree Publishing
PMB 59051
350 Fifth Avenue, 59th Floor
New York, New York 10118

Published in the United Kingdom
Crabtree Publishing
Maritime House
Basin Road North, Hove
BN41 1WR

Published in Australia
Crabtree Publishing
3 Charles Street
Coburg North
VIC 3058

Natural Resources Close-Up

Contents

We need natural resources

Think about the things you use every day. You read books. You walk on a sidewalk. You drink water and eat foods. Where do these things come from?

They come from natural resources! Natural resources are things in nature that people use. Trees give us paper. We grow food in soil. We drink clean water from lakes.

What is air?

When you blow up a balloon, what is it filled with? It is filled with air! You cannot see air, but air is all around you. You need air to breathe.

Air is another natural resource. We are always breathing air into our bodies. It keeps us alive. Air is made up of gases. A gas is something with no shape. It will fill up any space it is in.

Working together

Plants and people work together. Plants make their own food. Plants release a gas called **oxygen** into the air when they make food. People need oxygen to breathe.

People help plants by adding a gas to air that plants need! People breathe in and out. We breathe in oxygen and breathe out a gas called **carbon dioxide**. Plants take in carbon dioxide when they make food.

oxygen

carbon dioxide

Wonderful wind

Do you know why trees sway back and forth? Or why your kite flies? They are being blown by wind. Wind is moving air.

Wind can be gentle. It can ruffle your hair.
Wind can also be very strong. **Tornadoes**
and **hurricanes** are storms with strong winds.
They can destroy people's homes.

Helping plants grow

Air helps plants to grow! Air moves water around Earth. Wind blows clouds from place to place. Clouds carry rainwater that plants need to survive.

seeds

Wind also spreads plant **seeds**. Plant seeds are carried by the wind to new places. There they can grow into new plants.

Resources at risk

People are connected to Earth's natural resources. We need the air, land, and water around us to live. However, the actions of people can damage our natural resources.

People damage the air by creating **air pollution**. Air pollution is harmful chemicals in the air that make air unclean. Breathing unclean air makes people sick. As wind blows, air pollution is spread to more places.

Causes of air pollution

How do people create air pollution? The cars people drive create air pollution. Factories also create air pollution. Factories are buildings where products that people buy are made.

Many things in our homes, such as televisions, lights, fridges, and stoves need energy to run. Energy is also used to heat our homes. Most energy is produced in special factories which often create air pollution.

Take action!

Everyone can help reduce air pollution! Start by using less energy in your home. Turn off the lights in an empty room. Play outside instead of watching television. This way you will have fun and save energy!

What do you think?

Heating your home uses a lot of energy. What ways are these people staying warm instead of turning up the heat?

Use less

The fewer new products we buy, the less products factories have to make. This reduces, or cuts down, on air pollution. Try buying used products at garage sales or second-hand stores instead of buying new ones.

Borrowing books from the library is a good way to read books without having to buy new copies.

Earth's air cleaners

Did you know trees clean the air? Trees remove pollution from the air when they make food. Protecting trees also protects the air!

Paper is made from trees. Using less paper protects trees. Find fun ways to reuse paper instead of throwing it away.

What do you think?

How are these children helping to reduce air pollution?

Words to know

 **air pollution** 15, 16, 17, 18, 20, 21, 22, 23

 carbon dioxide 9

 hurricanes 11

 oxygen 8, 9

 **seeds** 13

tornadoes 11

Notes to adults and an activity

This hands-on activity allows children to see dust and other elements that pollute our air.

Materials
- four cue cards or pieces of white cardboard
- petroleum jelly
- plastic knife or tool to spread petroleum jelly on cards
- four zip-top sandwich bags
- a vacuum cleaner or broom, dusting cloths

Procedure
1. Use the knife to spread a thin layer of petroleum jelly on two cue cards.
2. Place one of the cards in a spot on the floor where it will not be in the way.
3. Place the other card on a desk or another hard surface.
4. Leave the cards there for two full days.
5. Observe the cards and have children comment on what they see trapped in the jelly.
6. Place each card in a sealed zip-top bag and save them.
7. Vacuum or sweep the room. Wipe surfaces to remove dust.
8. Repeat the experiment with the remaining two cards.

Observations
There will likely be dust from the air trapped in the petroleum jelly on the first two cards. Does one card have more dust than the other? How are the results different the second time? Is there more or less dust on the two new cards than there is on the cards you used before cleaning?

Conclusion
What does the amount of dust on the second set of cards tell you about the air after cleaning your room? Invite children to share their conclusions.

Learning More

Books
Rapping about: The air around us by Bobbie Kalman. Crabtree Publishing Company, 2012.
The Air We Breathe by Jen Green. Rosen Publishing Group, 2008.

Websites
This interactive site lets children control the amount of air pollution released into the environment to learn about the consequences. www.smogcity2.com/

This website has many kid-friendly links with helpful ways kids can help keep the air clean. www.sbcapcd.org/students.htm